A Writer

A Writer

M . B . G O F F S T E I N

Harper & Row, Publishers

Library of Congress Cataloging in Publication Data
Goffstein, M. B.
    A writer.

    "A Charlotte Zolotow book."
    Summary: What it means to be a writer—to be an
observer, a shaper, a collector of images gleaned from
the everyday world.
    1. Authorship—Juvenile literature.   2. Authors
—Juvenile literature.   [1. Authorship.   2. Authors]
I. Title.
PN153.G63 1984   811'.54   83-49488
ISBN 0-06-022142-9
ISBN 0-06-022143-7 (lib. bdg.)

Designed by Constance Fogler
1 2 3 4 5 6 7 8 9 10
First Edition

TO

Charlotte Zolotow

A Writer

A writer

sits on her couch,

holding an idea,

until it's time

to set words

upon paper,

to cut, prune,

plan, and shape them.

She is a gardener,

never sure

of her ground,

or of which seeds

are rooting there.

She has grown

flowers, weeds,

a slender tree.

Now she dreams

of pansies

and heart's-ease.

At first daylight,

she sees

two small green leaves

close to the soil.

If a rabbit eats them,

she's not mad at him.

She knows more

will grow,

for a writer

always studies,

looks, and listens.

Thoughts that open
in her heart,
and weather every mood
and change of mind,
she will care for.

She's only one
of many writers,
working alone
at her desk,
hoping her books

will spread the seeds
of ideas.

A CHARLOTTE ZOLOTOW BOOK